If Trees Could Talk

**Other books for young readers about the environment
from the Wisconsin Historical Society Press**

Learning from the Land: Wisconsin Land Use

Working with Water: Wisconsin Waterways

Digging and Discovery: Wisconsin Archaeology

If Trees Could Talk

Stories About Wisconsin Trees

R. Bruce Allison

Introduction by Paul DeLong

Wisconsin Historical Society Press

Published by the Wisconsin Historical Society Press
Publishers since 1855

© 2009 by the State Historical Society of Wisconsin

wisconsin**history**.org

Photographs identified with WHi or WHS are from the Society's collections; address requests to reproduce these photos to the Visual Materials Archivist at Wisconsin Historical Society, 816 State Street, Madison, WI 53706.

Front cover photo courtesy of Donald R. Blegen.
Back cover photos courtesy of B-Wolfgang Hoffman *(left)*; WHi Image ID 42573 *(middle)*; and the Wisconsin Department of Natural Resources (ca. 1955) *(right)*.

Printed in Canada
Designed by Nancy Warnecke, Moonlit Ink, Madison, Wisconsin 53726

13 12 11 10 09   1 2 3 4 5

Library of Congress Cataloging-in-Publication Data

Allison, R. Bruce.
    If trees could talk : stories about Wisconsin trees / R. Bruce Allison ; introduction by Paul DeLong.—1st ed.
        p. cm.
    Includes bibliographical references and index.
    ISBN 978-0-87020-419-7 (pbk. : alk. paper) 1. Trees—Wisconsin—Anecdotes—Juvenile literature. I. Title.
    SD383.3.U6A452 2008
    977.5—dc22
                            2008031032

Mixed Sources
Cert no. SW-COC-001271
© 1996 FSC
FSC

Dedicated to children, trees, and the stories waiting to be told.

Contents

To the Children of Wisconsin:

Trees are terrific! They help us in many ways. Some are in forests that clean our air and water, produce paper and lumber for making things we use each day, and provide places for us to play and homes for an incredible number of plants and animals. Other trees are on the job every day along streets, in parks, and in yards. They make our cities beautiful places to live, reduce noise, shade us from the summer sun, and reduce pollution.

The stories in *If Trees Could Talk* remind us how important trees are in our lives and in our State's history. The author, Bruce Allison, tells the trees' stories for them so that we can learn to love, respect, plant, protect, conserve, and value trees and the many benefits we receive from them.

As Wisconsin Chief Forester, my job is to look after our state's trees and forests. I work with people across the state to make sure trees are cared for in a way that enables them to grow and thrive, both today and long into the future. I hope that reading this book will inspire you to care for our trees and to listen for their stories.

Paul De Long

Wisconsin Chief Forester

Taliesin Elm

TREES AND PEOPLE NEED EACH OTHER

Trees are generous. They give us food such as apples, pears, bananas, almonds, walnuts, and maple syrup. They give us clean air and release oxygen for us to breathe. They provide shade to keep us cool on hot summer days. They create homes for many animals and plants.

Trees also give us important stories about our state of Wisconsin. This book is about those stories. People like trees and need all the things trees give us. But trees also need people. Trees are alive, so they can be hurt or killed by thoughtless actions. Digging holes under trees hurts their roots. Cutting into the bark wounds a tree's bark or "skin." Breaking branches makes it hard for a tree to grow and stay healthy.

You can keep trees healthy by protecting them from harm. In the future you can also help by planting new trees. That way, children will have new tree stories to tell. You probably have a favorite tree story of your own!

The General MacArthur White Pine in 1946. Can you see the people at the base of the tree?

ANCIENT AND HUGE TREES

General MacArthur White Pine
Nicolet National Forest

The General MacArthur White Pine was the tallest white pine in the world, and one of the oldest. Thousands of tourists came to the Nicolet National Forest to see this 400-year-old tree. The towering tree reminded them of General Douglas MacArthur. General MacArthur was one of America's best-known war heroes. He was in charge of the American soldiers in the Pacific during World War II. Like the tree, the general was powerful and commanding.

A parade welcomed General MacArthur back home after World War II.

The General MacArthur White Pine was discovered by a U.S. forest ranger in 1945. The pine's huge roots had openings large enough for small animals to live in. Its piney top was home to many kinds of birds. The tree showed us how northern Wisconsin must have looked before the lumberjacks got to work with their axes. From just this one tree, there was enough wood to build an entire house!

But root disease, decay, and lightning strikes made the tree weak. In 2003, the MacArthur Pine burned to the ground. No one knows if it was struck by lightning or if somebody set fire to it. Either way, one of Wisconsin's oldest and largest trees is gone.

The Buried Forest
Pleasant Prairie

Along the shores of Lake Michigan just south of Kenosha, there's a buried forest. The forest is in an area called the Southport Dunes. Dunes are huge hills made of sand. The Southport Dunes reach all the way to the shore of the lake, where waves of water hit them again and again. Over time, the waves washed away enough sand to uncover the roots and branches of trees. These trees were part of a forest that grew there more than 6,000 years ago.

In 1961, scientists found tree stumps stuck in 12 inches of black mud and clay. The scientists identified these ancient trees as oak, elm, and ash. Now, their wood is black and spongy. It used to be green and firm.

Studying the buried trees is important. The types of pollen still in the logs can tell us about the kinds of plants that grew in Wisconsin thousands of years ago.

Brule River White Pine
Brule River State Forest

For centuries, an ancient white pine grew in a protected spot in the Brule River State Forest. Its trunk was more than 18 feet around!

The tree grew near a well-known private vacation spot called Cedar Island Estate. Many famous people stayed there. President Calvin Coolidge was one of them. In 1926, the president set up a summer White House at Cedar Island Estate so he could fish and relax.

President Coolidge went fishing on the Brule River in the summer of 1928.

Cedar Island, a quiet vacation spot on the Brule River.

Two men gaze up at the Brule River White Pine in 1962.

In the early 1980s, one of the tree's largest limbs broke off. It barely missed the people working below! The man who owned the tree knew it needed help. He asked Wisconsin tree doctor Bruce Allison to come and heal the tree. He climbed 120 feet up the trunk past the squirrels, porcupines, and eagles' nests. That's as high as a building 12 stories tall! Bruce Allison used his chainsaw to cut away the dead and dangerous branches. The great pine lived for a while longer, but it finally died from its wounds and old age.

Columbus Cottonwood

Columbus

A prize-winning cottonwood tree stands on John Crombie's farm in Columbus. Its trunk is more than 26 feet around! It would take you and eight of your friends with your arms outstretched to reach all the way around it.

John Crombie had lived on the farm his entire life. His father and grandfather farmed the land before he was born. Even so, John didn't know his tree was that large. One morning, he read in the local paper that another tree claimed to be the biggest. He decided to go out and see for himself. He took a rope and a measuring stick with him, and went out to measure his tree. Then he sent the measurement to Wisconsin's Champion Tree Program. Although the wind has broken many large branches from the tree, it is still one of our state's largest trees.

For more than 100 years, this amazing tree was hidden in Mr. Crombie's backyard. In 1980, when the book *Wisconsin's Champion Trees* was published, the tree became famous. Its photo was on the cover of the book.

John Crombie and his son stand next to the base or trunk of the huge Columbus Cottonwood.

UNUSUAL TREES

The Scary Oak

Kettle Moraine State Forest

There's a spooky tree growing along the nature trail in Kettle Moraine State Forest. It is an old bur oak, monstrous in size and appearance. The Scary Oak looks like a corkscrew because its branches and twigs grow crooked and twisted.

The sign in front of the Scary Oak tells us why the tree is so twisted. It has big knots of wood that grow on the tree like warts, called burls. Burls are created when insects or fungus get underneath the bark. Burls can make a tree useless for timber and impossible to split into firewood. But the tough and wavy-grained burls are used by artists, who make them into bowls and other objects.

ELIZABETH DEAKMAN

Can you see scary faces in the Scary Oak?

WHS MUSEUM 1985.109.10

Artist Harry Nohr made this burl bowl.

Harry Nohr was one such artist from Mineral Point, Wisconsin. When he created his burl bowls, he said, "Trees are a lot like people. A tree is a lot prettier if it had to struggle to grow." Crafting these beautiful bowls from the knotted wood was also a struggle. It took Henry up to two years to finish just one of his amazing creations.

Upside-Down Trees
Wilmot

People used to say that the two weeping elms in a front yard in Wilmot looked as though they had been planted upside down. But they weren't. Two different types of elm were joined together to make this unusual looking tree. You can still see the place where the two trees were joined together. It looks like a swollen ring halfway up the trunk of the tree.

PHIL SANDER (1963)

Can you see the ring halfway up the Upside-Down Trees?

These trees are called Camperdown elm. The name comes from a tree that grew at the Camperdown House near Dundee, Scotland. Camperdown elms have branches that hang down like long vines and flat tops.

"Upside-down trees" were popular around 1900. Some still grow in the lawns of old mansions and hospitals.

The Haunted Mansion and Pines

Merrill

The Scott's Mansion in Merrill is surrounded by tall white pines. Some people still think the mansion and the hill it stands on are haunted. Before the mansion was built, an Indian chief buried his lovely daughter Jenny on that hill. She died from an illness brought to the Indians by the early lumberjacks. The chief warned that bad things would happen to anyone who did not leave her grave alone.

In 1883, Merrill's first mayor, T. B. Scott, started to build his mansion on top of the hill. But as soon as construction started, T. B. Scott died. His wife continued building the mansion. The next year, she also died. That same year, the Scotts' son was murdered by the architect! The two of them had argued about whether the hill was haunted. Bad things continued to take

M. N. TAYLOR (1981).

One of the Scott's Mansion pines in 1981.

place. One owner went missing, and was never heard from again. Another man who lived in the mansion took a vacation to England in 1912. He sailed on a ship called the Titanic. He lost his life, along with many other passengers, when the ship hit an iceberg.

Finally, the mansion was given to a group of nuns in 1923. No one has died a strange death since. At last, the white pines are growing in peace.

The Durand Hanging Tree stood right next to the courthouse.

Durand Courthouse Hanging Tree

Durand

During pioneer times, some trees were used as hanging trees. When a person committed a very serious crime, a judge might sentence that person to death by hanging. But sometimes the people of the community did not wait for the judge to decide. That's what happened in the town of Durand.

On November 19, 1881, Ed Williams and his brother Lon shot dead two sheriffs who had come to arrest them. When Ed was brought to the courthouse, an angry crowd overpowered his guards. They threw a hangman's noose over his head, and dragged him outside. Then they hanged him on an oak next to the Durand courthouse. It was a shameful act, and no way to use a tree.

Parade Day Hanging Tree

La Crosse

On October 16, 1884, Frank Burton was marching at the front of a parade in La Crosse. Hundreds of people stood along the street and watched. Suddenly, a man in the crowd, Scotty Mitchell, raised a gun, fired, and shot Frank down.

Scotty was immediately taken to jail. But some people weren't willing to wait for a judge to decide if Scotty should live or die. A mob of angry people formed. They forced their way into the jail. They dragged Scotty outside and hanged him from an oak tree by the courthouse.

The next day, newspaper articles called the oak the Hanging Tree. City officials ordered it to be cut down. They did not want the public to remember that a mob had broken the law and killed a man without a trial.

Trail Marker Trees

PHIL SANDER (1962)

Twin Lakes Trail Marker Tree

Some people think that Indians or early settlers may have bent trees to make them point toward important places. Others disagree. Whether or not the stories are true, many tales were told about these oddly shaped trees.

One trail marker tree was found at Twin Lakes in Kenosha County near the top of a high ridge. It pointed south toward the land between the two lakes. Another trail marker tree stood in Madison near West High School. It was a hickory that marked the crossing of two trails. Its twisted branches looked as though they pointed in four different directions.

Another trail marker tree that has vanished is a beech tree that stood on a street corner in Milwaukee. Someone had cut an Indian figure holding a bow and arrow into the trunk. The arrow pointed to the Menominee River.

Mercer's Addition Trail Marker Tree

WHI IMAGE ID 42573

INDIAN STORY TREES

Neenah Treaty Elm

Neenah

An amazing elm used to stand at the mouth of the Fox River near Neenah. It was called the Neenah Treaty Elm. It marked the place where chiefs of Indian tribes met together. Under its great branches, the chiefs made treaties, or agreements, about using land and water.

The Indian people also watched over the land as settlers and soldiers started to travel through Wisconsin Territory. In 1819, a Ho-Chunk Indian chief named Four Legs stood under the Treaty Elm. A group of soldiers approached him in a boat. At the head of the boat was their leader, Henry Leavenworth.

"You cannot go forward," said Chief Four Legs to Leavenworth. He wanted to protect the land from white settlers. "The lake is locked."

WHI IMAGE ID 41695

Neenah Treaty Elm

WHI IMAGE ID 41697

Governor Doty's cabin, where wood from the Neenah Treaty Elm was made into a table.

Leavenworth stood up in his boat. He lifted his rifle high and cried, "So! The lake is locked. Then here is the key in my hand." He said to Four Legs, "I will unlock the lake and go on."

Leavenworth aimed his gun at Four Legs. The Indian had no choice. "Very well," he said. "You may pass through."

The Neenah Treaty Elm stood until 1890. That's when it was taken down to make the river wider so boats could pass through. The tree is gone, but it hasn't been forgotten. A slab from its wood has been made into a tabletop in Governor James Doty's old cabin in Neenah.

Indian Half-Way Tree
Brodhead

In the 1800s, Indians passed north along the Sugar River each spring. Some were in canoes. Others rode horses or walked. A large bur oak marked the point halfway between Lake Michigan and the Mississippi River. The Half-Way Tree was a favorite camping spot for Native people and later for settlers.

RICH RYGH, *THE CAPITAL TIMES*

You can still see Indian Half-Way Tree in Green County.

Around 1867, the family who owned the land where the tree stood said an Indian chief came to their door. The chief pointed to the tree and said it should never be cut down. It never has been. You can still see it today on Highway 81 in Green County.

Today, experts are still amazed at how accurate the tree is. It is only 6 miles from the actual half-way point between Lake Michigan and the Mississippi River.

Blackhawk Hickory
Madison

Chief Black Hawk, painted by Robert M. Sully in 1832.

In the 1800s, settlers moved across the United States from east to west. As settlers moved, Indian nations were pushed further and further west from their villages. In 1832, a Sauk leader named Black Hawk and 1200 of his followers were unhappy in the land west of the Mississippi where they were pushed. They crossed back over the river to return to their village in what is now Illinois. When they got there, they found non-Indians settled there. Black Hawk realized that he and his followers could not stay. But settlers were afraid of the Indians, and soldiers fired on Black Hawk's people. This was the beginning of what came to be known as the Black Hawk War.

Black Hawk and his people could not get back across the Mississippi. Soldiers chased Black Hawk and his followers up through southwest Wisconsin. Around the land that became Madison, soldiers followed the Indians past the southern shores of Lake Mendota. They passed by a big shagbark hickory. The hickory became known as the Blackhawk Hickory. The land around it later became the Blackhawk Country Club.

B-WOLFGANG HOFFMANN (1979)

Black Hawk Hickory

WHI IMAGE ID 42502

Black Hawk Cottonwood

The Black Hawk War ended very badly for the Indian leader and his followers. When they finally reached the Mississippi at Bad Axe (north of Prairie du Chien), soldiers fired on them as they tried to cross. Only 150 people and Black Hawk survived. The U.S. government used the Black Hawk War as a way to get land for new settlers to what became Wisconsin.

Some citizens of Prairie du Chien believed that Black Hawk once hid in a hollow trunk of a giant cottonwood tree. The Blackhawk Cottonwood was a reminder of Chief Black Hawk's bravery and his attempt to help his people. But in 1930, the tree fell during a windstorm.

Indian Agency House and Elms
Portage

A very old elm stands guard near the entrance of the Indian Agency House in Portage. The house was built in 1832 for John Kinzie. He was the Indian agent at Fort Winnebago. Indian agents worked for the United States government. They helped make treaties between the U.S. government and Native people. Good agents like John Kinzie also worked hard to help the Indians get along with the non-Indian settlers.

WHI IMAGE ID 42727

The Indian Agency House was surrounded by tall elms.

When he was younger, John worked for the American Fur Company in Prairie du Chien. He learned Indian customs and languages. These skills came in handy. John often helped Indians and settlers to talk with one another. In 1830, he became an Indian agent to the Ho-Chunk tribe.

Juliette and John Kinzie

John and his wife, Juliette, traveled by steamboat from Detroit to Green Bay. Then they took a boat up the Fox River to Fort Winnebago. Juliette brought all of her belongings with her—even a piano! She wrote about her Wisconsin adventures in a book called *Wau-Bun*. Wau-Bun means "early morning" in Ho-Chunk.

When John and Juliette moved into their new house, the first thing they did was plant the dooryard elm.

A fur trader talks with a circle of Indians inside their teepee.

PIONEER TREES

A painting of the Peck cabin by Isabella Dengel.

WHI IMAGE ID 2859

Peck Bur Oak

Madison

In 1837, Eben and Rosaline Peck built a cabin on the shores of Lake Monona. They were the first settlers to build their home in what would soon become Wisconsin's capital, Madison. They chose to build their cabin beneath the sturdy limbs of a great bur oak.

Eben arrived first in the winter of 1837 to start building the cabin. He called for his pregnant wife Rosaline and four-year-old son, Victor, to join him. Rosaline came from their farm in Blue Mounds 29 miles away. She and Victor traveled through thick snow and past howling wolves. Finally, they arrived at the log cabin.

Rosaline quickly went to work turning the rough cabin into a real home. Guests could sit in the shade of the bur oak to have a cup of coffee, or they could share a delicious meal of venison or muskrat stew. They talked about the building of the state capitol nearby. That spring, Rosaline gave birth to a baby girl. She was the first child born to settlers in Madison. Her parents named her Wisconsoniana.

WHI IMAGE ID 3941

Rosaline Peck

The Peck cabin was destroyed in 1857. In 1930, the oak was cut down make room for an office building. Standing near the building is a plaque that tells the history of the tree and cabin. It is all that is left of the Peck's story.

Dunbar Oak
Waukesha

Richard Dunbar decided to make Waukesha his home when a tree saved his life. In August 1868, he became very ill while traveling. He was sure he was about to die. Richard sat down beneath a gentle white oak to rest. He drank from a spring of water bubbling up nearby. Soon he felt miraculously refreshed. He called the tree his "guardian angel."

A postcard of Bethesda Spring after it became famous.

Richard was sure the water from the spring had cured him. He bought the land around the tree and began to sell the spring water. The water became a popular cure for many sicknesses. It was so popular, in fact, that the town of Waukesha became famous. People came to Waukesha from all over the United States hoping to be healed.

Richard lived for another ten years, but the tree survived until 1991. That's when a 100-mile-per-hour wind blew it down. A count of the tree's rings showed that it was 320 years old. That must have been very healthy water!

Walking Staff Tree

Lake Delton

Back in 1848, some families made the long journey from New England to Wisconsin in covered wagons. They hoped to find cheap land that was good to farm. The Tinkham family from Vermont was one such family. Along the way, Joseph Tinkham cut a branch from a cottonwood tree. He used it as a walking staff to help him on the journey. When he got to their new farm between Lake Delton and Reedsburg, he pushed the staff into the ground. There it grew into a big tree.

One hundred years later, the owner of the land gave the land on which the tree stood to Wisconsin. It was turned into a roadside park, where visitors could see the Walking Staff Tree. But the tree attracted lightning as well as visitors. Eventually, the tree became unsafe. It was taken down.

A man named Vernon Harrison saved a piece of the old cottonwood. He planted a shoot from the roots of the tree in his front yard. That shoot grew into a strong, beautiful tree. The tree is a living symbol of one pioneer family's covered wagon journey to Wisconsin.

Wyalusing Maple
Wyalusing State Park

The Wyalusing Giant Maple stood guard over the Mississippi and Wisconsin Rivers.

The Wyalusing Maple was a watchful giant of a tree. It grew at Signal Point above the spot where the Mississippi and Wisconsin rivers join together. From Signal Point, the tree watched the coming and going of American Indians, explorers, soldiers, and settlers. It also watched the migration of the passenger pigeon, a beautiful bird that flew in flocks so large that they seemed to fill the sky. Sadly, when the forests were cut down by the settlers for farmland, the birds lost their homes and source of food. Settlers shot many of these birds for food or sport. Passenger pigeons finally disappeared altogether, becoming extinct in 1914.

COURTESY OF THE WISCONSIN DEPARTMENT OF NATURAL RESOURCES

The passenger pigeon memorial.

Just a few years later, in 1917, Signal Point became part of Wyalusing State Park. Now, the trees and animals are protected. If you go to the park, you can hike to the place where the Wyalusing Maple used to stand. You can also visit the monument made to remember the passenger pigeons.

WHI IMAGE ID 34684

Delavan Founder's Oak
Delavan

Samuel Phoenix was one of Wisconsin's early pioneers. On the night of July 2, 1836, he wrote in his journal that he slept under a magnificent bur oak tree. At the time, he was on an exploring trip in Wisconsin Territory. A short time later, Samuel started a sawmill on Lake Delavan. There, workers used machines to turn logs into planks. The planks could be used to construct houses, barns, and other buildings. A town named Delavan was built up around the sawmill. The next year Samuel brought his family to Wisconsin from New York.

This is what Delavan looked like in 1905.

WHI IMAGE ID 30377

This is the bur oak Samuel Phoenix slept under.

The tree Samuel slept under still stands. It is now thought to be more than 400 years old.

Cram/Houghton Blaze Tree

Trout Lake

Not all the people who came to Wisconsin Territory from the East Coast were explorers, lumberjacks, or fur traders. Many were surveyors. Surveyors measured the size and shape of land very carefully so they could draw maps of large areas. One of their jobs was to draw boundary lines. Boundary lines showed where one territory ended and another began.

Thomas Jefferson Cram was one such surveyor. He made maps by walking across the land and taking careful notes and measurements. Thomas came to Wisconsin Territory in 1841 on a mission to check an earlier mapmaker's work. The earlier map was not quite right. He brought an engineer named Douglass Houghton along to help.

The men had a big job to do. They had to map a boundary line more than 100 miles long! The boundary line was between Wisconsin Territory and Michigan. It was very far north, far from the places most settlers lived. The work was hard and long, and took many months.

Can you make out the date under the men's names?

Years later, in 1866, a discovery was made at Trout Lake in Vilas County. Carved into the bark of a large pine tree growing on the lakeshore were the men's names and a date. They had passed by the spot more than 20 years earlier!

The trunk with the carved words was saved when the tree was cut down. Visit it at the Wisconsin Historical Museum in Madison.

Thomas Cram helped create this map of Wisconsin and Michigan in 1868.

Grignon Elms

Kaukauna

The tall elms planted around the Grignon mansion in Kaukauna help us remember one of Wisconsin's earliest and most important families. The Grignon family descended from French kings and queens. In the 1700s, the family came from France to the United States. They helped to start one of the first fur trading settlements in Wisconsin, at Kaukauna, in 1760.

In 1837, Charles Grignon built a 12-room, three-story house on the banks of the Fox River. He brought workers all the way from New York to help build the house! It soon became known as "The Mansion in the Woods." The mansion was the Grignon family home for almost 100 years. The last of the Grignon family moved out of the home in 1933.

The Grignon House is now a historic site that you can visit. Sadly, most of the elms planted by Charles died from Dutch elm disease in the 1970s.

The "Mansion in the Woods" was surrounded by elms.

CIVIL WAR TREES

. . . .

Civil War Sign-Up Tree
Delavan

The Civil War was a hard time for Wisconsin families. Many young men from small towns across the state decided to fight to keep the United States from being divided into 2 countries. Young men signed up to be soldiers under the shade of large, leafy trees. One of these sign-up trees is still alive at the corner of Seventh and Washington streets in the town of Delavan. From 1861 to 1865, new soldiers would gather under the bur oak before they boarded trains. They were headed for training camps such as Camp Randall in Madison. A giant grapevine used to grow beside the tree and wrap up in its branches. Children loved to swing from it. Today a parking lot surrounds the tree. A bronze marker reminds people of its historic past.

During the Civil War, men signed up for battle under this tree's branches.
(inset) Knut Iverson was a Wisconsin soldier killed in the Civil War.

The President's Oak at the University of Wisconsin-Madison.

President's Oak

Madison

According to legend, Civil War soldiers at Camp Randall in Madison used a big oak tree on Observatory Hill to practice shooting. The oak, called the President's Tree, is on the campus of the University of Wisconsin in Madison. To this day, you can still see large wounds in the trunk of the tree.

Harvey Oak

Madison

WHI IMAGE ID 5601

Camp Randall was a busy training ground for soldiers in 1861.

The Harvey Oak grew at Camp Randall in Madison, where soldiers trained for battle. The oak was named after Louis Powell Harvey. He was the governor of Wisconsin during the Civil War. Governor Harvey traveled south where he visited wounded Wisconsin soldiers. Sadly, Governor Harvey stepped and slipped between two steamboats. He fell in the water between the boats and drowned in the Tennessee River. His body was found 60 miles downstream.

WHI IMAGE ID 37904

MARY FRANCES SCHJONBERG (1976)

The Harvey Oak at Camp Randall in 1976.
(inset) Louis Powell Harvey was a young governor.

After the war, the Harvey hospital was turned into an orphanage.

Cordelia Harvey carried on with her husband's work after he died.

His wife, Cordelia Harvey, was very sad when she learned of her husband's death. Even so, she decided to continue his work. She visited all the military hospitals along the Mississippi River but became upset when she saw their unhealthy conditions. Cordelia went to see President Lincoln in Washington, D.C. She demanded that the wounded soldiers be allowed to return to their own states. She knew they would get better care near their own homes. At first the president said no. But Cordelia did not give up.

Finally, President Lincoln agreed to let the wounded men go home. He also helped to build better hospitals for soldiers. The first hospital for soldiers was built in Madison on the shores of Lake Monona. It was named the Harvey Hospital. After the war the hospital became home to children whose parents died during the war.

Cordelia Harvey is a true Wisconsin hero. She deserves to have a tree named after her, too.

Grant County Sycamore

Bloomington

One of Wisconsin's largest sycamore trees grows in Grant County on Sycamore Road. This sycamore is a living reminder of the terrible price of war. A group of seventh- and eighth-grade students at the North Andover school near Bloomington uncovered its story. They discovered that the tree had been planted by an early settler, Joseph Crain Orr. During the Civil War, Joseph learned that his son had been taken prisoner in the South. Joseph had to travel more than a thousand miles to search for him. He found his son in a Tennessee hospital. The young soldier had been in prison for a long time. He was weak from his wounds, and died in his father's arms.

Joseph Orr returned his son's body to Wisconsin along with a young tree he found along the way. He planted the sycamore sapling beside his son's grave. It is a living memory of his son's service during the Civil War.

B·WOLFGANG HOFFMANN (1979)

Grant County Sycamore

29

WELL-LOVED TREES

Montello Cottonwood
Montello

One of the most famous trees in Wisconsin is the Montello Cottonwood. This giant tree is probably 200 to 300 years old. That means it was standing when the French explorers passed through Wisconsin. The tree was already large when the first settlers came in 1844.

Montello Cottonwood

MARY FRANCES SCHJONBERG (1982)

The tree is just a block from downtown Montello. Those who live or work near the tree love to look at its beauty through all four seasons.

One of its biggest fans was Robert L. Wright. He worked for the newspaper in Montello. Robert could see the tree from his office window, and he grew to love it. He said, "For 30 years, I worked in my newspaper shop directly across the street from the cottonwood. Never a day went by that I did not look and admire. The tree was—and is—my friend."

Tea Circle Oaks

Spring Green

Frank Lloyd Wright was a very famous American architect. He believed that the natural world—trees, hills, and rivers—should be part of the design of every building. Mr. Wright was born and lived in Wisconsin. In 1911, he built his home in Spring Green, called Taliesin. It was also a school for architecture students.

In the courtyard of Taliesin, Mr. Wright built a "tea circle" around an old oak tree. The tree's arms seemed to reach out to gather people beneath its branches. Under its shade, Mr. Wright would gather his students for midmorning tea breaks and interesting conversations. They called it the Tree Circle Oak.

After Mr. Wright died in 1959, the tree was struck by lightning. Another oak nearby became the new Tea Circle Oak. People met under its great branches. That tree lived until a windstorm brought it down in 1998. It had to be removed limb by limb from the roof of Taliesin by tree doctor Bruce Allison. Today, yet another Tea Circle Oak has been planted with the hope that it will grow for another 200 years.

WHI IMAGE ID 35055

Can you spot two Tea Circle Oaks in this picture?

WHI IMAGE ID 1921

Frank Lloyd Wright

Boscobel's Dean Oak

Boscobel

The 300-year-old Dean Oak near Boscobel is famous. Its portrait has been painted and hangs in the Boscobel Public Library. It was made famous when its owner "set it free." He did this by giving the tree the land on which it stood!

The tree was already large and beautiful when Charles K. Dean, who founded the town of Boscobel, bought the land. He grew very fond of the wonderful tree. Then Charles sold part of the farm to John Verrill, a horse trader. He told John that the tree must never be harmed. He insisted that the tree must have a third of an acre all its own.

Bascobel's Dean Oak

This old oak has seen a lot of history. It grows next to Homer Road, which was once an Indian trail. The Indian trail connected Galena, Illinois, with Prairie du Chien, Wisconsin. Many groups of pioneers and Indians stopped beneath the tree's pleasant shade to talk, play a game, or rest.

Today the Dean Oak is not as large and grand as it once was. It has lost some of its branches to lightning and windstorms. But it is still alive and free, growing on the land that belongs to it.

NORRIS LINDERUD (1955)

Can you see the way the Hanerville Oak stood in the middle of the road?

Hanerville Oak

Hanerville

A large, beautiful bur oak tree used to stand like a police officer directing traffic in the middle of a street in Hanerville. Children in the one-room schoolhouse nearby loved the tree. Their teacher would tell them the story of how it was saved when the street was made wider in 1934.

A man named Tharon Miller led the fight to save the oak. He reminded the town that it had been a very important tree for early settlers. They used it to mark the road between Janesville and Madison. Settlers knew they were on the right road when they passed beneath its branches.

Sadly, the tree is no longer there. Now people in their cars will not need to worry about bumping into a tree growing in the middle of the road. They will never know that they are driving where a historic tree once stood.

Rhodes Bald Cypress
Richard Bong State Recreational Area

John Rhodes liked to plant unusual trees on his family farm in Kenosha County. He was also a very strict father. When his youngest daughter, Mary, wanted to be married, John said no. His daughter ran away to marry her sweetheart, and they moved far, far away—all the way to Louisiana. Angry at being disobeyed, John ordered the rest of the family never to write letters to Mary again. But, of course, they did it anyway.

A year later, Mary wrote to tell her family that she was going to have a baby. Her father finally came to his senses. He traveled all the way to Louisiana to make up with his daughter and greet his new grandchild. He brought back a bald cypress sapling from Louisiana. He planted it in his farmyard as a reminder of his reunion with his daughter.

WALLY E. SCHULZ (1962)

Phil Sanders measuring the Rhodes Bald Cypress in 1962.

The bald cypress is a tree not usually found in Wisconsin, and it had a very funny feature. At the bottom, the tree grew "knees": woody knobs that grew up from the tree's roots like big, bony knees. The tree's knees made it hard for the family to cut the grass around the tree. But no matter how often they were cut down, the trees knees grew back.

The Rhodes bald cypress had a hard time of it during the bitter cold Wisconsin winters. It grows best in warm places like Louisiana. Often, the family would come outside on winter mornings to find cracks in the trunk big enough to fit a mittened hand inside! But over time, these cracks healed, and the tree survived.

That tree still grows where John planted it. Now it is 50 feet tall and more than 150 years old! It is a monument to the power of family love and forgiveness.

Rhodes Bald Cypress

The Jones Dairy Farm from above, in 1934.

Centennial Maple

Fort Atkinson

In 1876, a silver maple was planted on the Jones dairy farm near Fort Atkinson to celebrate the nation's 100th birthday. That's when it was given a special name: the Centennial Maple. Centennial is a word like century, meaning 100 years.

The farm was first given to Milo Jones as payment for his work as a Wisconsin surveyor in the 1830s. He planted the Centennial Maple in 1876. In 1976, 100 years later, Milo's great-great-grandson, Edward, planted seedlings from the Centennial Maple to celebrate the nation's 200th birthday.

Six generations of Joneses have lived on the farm. The Centennial Maple is a symbol of the family's pride and faith in their ancestors, their home, their state, and their country.

Centennial Maple

Pleasant Company Oak

Middleton

An ancient bur oak stands tall and graceful on the front lawn of the American Girl company in Middleton, Wisconsin. It was a special tree for the company founder, Pleasant Rowland. She used to look at the tree through her office window. Its strength and beauty inspired her as

Pleasant Company Oak

she worked. Pleasant used to be a teacher. Her dream was to create books and dolls for young girls that would tell the history of growing up female in America.

Today, the great bur oak still grows outside the company headquarters.

Joyce Kilmer's Tree Poem

One of the most famous poems about trees was written in 1913 by a young man named Joyce Kilmer. His full name was Alfred Joyce Kilmer. America loved the poem. Many schoolchildren could recite it from memory.

Joyce was from New York, but he loved to visit Wisconsin. He spent time at Campion College in Prairie du Chien. He even delivered a speech there at graduation, right before World War I. He wore his military uniform when he gave the speech, because he was going to be a soldier. Before Joyce sailed to Europe, he made a promise. He said he would move to Wisconsin when he returned from the war. Sadly, it was

Joyce Kilmer

a promise he could not keep. Joyce was killed in battle and buried in France. He never again saw the beautiful Wisconsin trees he loved so much. But his poem lives on:

Trees

I think that I shall never see
A poem lovely as a tree.

A tree whose lovely mouth is prest
Against the sweet earth's flowing breast.

A tree that looks at God all day,
And lifts her leafy arms to pray;

A tree that may in summer wear
A nest of robins in her hair.

Upon whose bosom snow has lain;
Who intimately lives with rain.

Poems are made by fools like me,
But only God can make a tree.

DISAPPEARING TREES

WHI IMAGE ID 1814

The last elm on State Street in Madison was cut down in 1974.

Remember the Elms

Madison

A hundred years ago, most streets in Wisconsin were lined with beautiful elm trees. Elms grew fast and tall. Their leafy branches touched high above the street and formed a shady arch. Drivers and walkers were kept cool on hot summer days. Elm trees kept people feeling cozy and safe at all times of the year.

People loved their elms so much that they planted more and more. But having so many elms wasn't a good thing. People forgot that having many different kinds of trees is healthier for all trees. The great elms seemed strong until a new disease came over from Europe.

The disease was called Dutch elm disease, and it spread like wildfire across Wisconsin. The legs of a tiny insect called the elm bark beetle carried Dutch elm disease. People tried to stop the insect. People also tried to treat the trees with medicine. But Dutch elm disease spread and finally killed most of the elms in Wisconsin cities and in other cities across America. The shady, elm-lined streets became history.

Gene Smalley, on the right, watches as Prince Philip plants a disease-fighting elm.

FOX PHOTOS LTD

Dutch elm disease moved on to the countryside. There, it struck down trees that shaded farmers working in the fields. That's when Gene Smalley, a Wisconsin scientist, had an idea: Why not find an elm tree that could fight against disease? A tree like this could take the place of all of the dead elms. Mr. Smalley worked hard for many years. Finally, he succeeded. His disease-fighting elm became famous around the world. The royal family of England asked Mr. Smalley to come to their home at Windsor Castle. They wanted him to plant one of his Wisconsin elms.

Lunde Chestnut Trees

Trempealeau

American Chestnut

Just like the elm tree, the chestnut was once an American favorite. It grew up and down the East Coast, from New York all the way down to Georgia. Then about 100 years ago, a deadly disease called chestnut blight killed most of the trees. This blight was a disease caused by a fungus infected by a virus. The fungus got underneath the trees' bark, killing them from the inside out.

Believe it or not, some chestnuts today are alive and well in Wisconsin. They are some of the only pure American chestnuts left in the world. A large grove of them grows in western Wisconsin on the farm of Einar Lunde, east of Trempealeau. Many of the trees are almost 100 years old. During the years of the blight, these trees were far away, protected from the disease. But recently, the blight has been discovered in some Wisconsin trees.

Chestnut trees are valued for their beauty, strong wood, and delicious nuts. Scientists are hard at work. They hope to grow a chestnut tree that can fight against disease, just like Mr. Smalley did for the elms.

SAVED TREES

· ·

Ben Logan's Big Maple

Seneca

Ben Logan and his family loved their towering maple.

Author Ben Logan has many memories about growing up on a small Wisconsin farm. In 1975, he wrote a book about his childhood called *The Land Remembers*. In it, he tells the story of a big soft maple growing next to his family home. The tree was very special to the family. It was the first tree they could see when they came home after a long journey. Its tall branches rose high above the hill that sheltered the farmhouse from wind. The family felt that the tree could tell when spring was coming. It bloomed a full week ahead of all the other trees. Ben's mother loved the tree. She would often sing as she looked up at its swaying limbs.

B-WOLFGANG HOFFMANN (1982)

But the maple was standing in a dangerous spot. It was right in the path of the wind. Its tall branches were made of soft, spongy wood. During a harsh windstorm, several limbs were blown from the tree onto the house. One just missed knocking down the chimney! Ben's father was firm. He said the tree would have to be cut down. Bens's brother and one of the hired hands set to work sharpening a big saw. But just as they started to cut into the bark, they stopped. They couldn't bear to cut it any further. Ben's mother and the children also refused to help cut it down. No one wanted for the tree to be cut down. Finally, Ben's father gave in.

The tree never was cut down, though it still has a scar from the blade of the saw. It is still growing today in Crawford County.

The Poet's Larch
Dodgeville

Edna Meudt was a Wisconsin poet. She dearly loved the trees on her Iowa County farm. She especially loved the huge larch tree in her front yard. It stood as high as an eight-story building, taller than any of the other trees. On a Saturday in 1973, a tornado swept through the farm. It pulled the larch up by its roots and threw it all the way across the road! Edna was determined to save the 100-year-old tree.

She called her friend, Reid Gilbert, for help. He was a teacher at the Valley Studio Mime School. On Sunday, he brought 26 students to Edna's farm to help clean up the storm damage. Some students laughed when Edna said she wanted to save the larch tree. But one student didn't. He said he was half Crow Indian. He warned that they must let the tree spirit know that help was coming or the spirit would leave the tree. At his request, Edna and the students ripped a bedsheet into strips and tied them to the roots of the tree. Then they covered the roots with a blanket and watered it well.

The Poet's Larch, after it was saved.

On Monday, a crane arrived to help replant tree. Edna said, "The strips tied to the tree's roots waved crazily in a rising wind." Although the tree had little chance of surviving, survive it did. The tree's spirit had not left. The larch put out new needles the next spring in a beautiful display of its will to live.

KEEPING TREES GREEN

The Sugar Maple
Wisconsin's State Tree

Wisconsin's state tree is the sugar maple. It was picked as a favorite by school children all the way back in 1893! But the sugar maple didn't become the official state tree until 1949. That's when a second vote was taken. Once again, the sugar maple was the favorite. It had more votes than the oak, pine, and elm.

Why did the kids choose the sugar maple? Maybe it was because of the cool shade it offers in the summer or the bright red leaves in the autumn. Or maybe they chose the sugar maple because it gives us delicious maple syrup for our morning pancakes. No matter why, it was a good choice. Wisconsin can be proud of our many sugar maple trees.

WISCONSIN DEPARTMENT OF TOURISM

A Wisconsin Sugar Maple

Students from Weston School in Cazenovia help tree doctor Trevor Lancaster place soil around the base of a tree on Arbor Day in 2005.

Arbor Day

Arbor Day is the day we celebrate the beauty and goodness of trees. It is an American holiday that started in Nebraska in 1872. That year, people in Nebraska planted more than a million trees. They hoped to keep the soil from blowing away in the strong wind. In Wisconsin, we celebrate Arbor Day on the last Friday in April.

Each Arbor Day, schoolchildren across the state spend the day learning about how trees grow. They learn what products come from the forest and why city trees are so important. Of course, no Arbor Day would be complete without planting a tree. Planting a tree today will make a better tomorrow.

Aldo Leopold's Good Oak

Baraboo

Aldo Leopold was one of the very first scientists to try to understand how plants, animals, and the environment worked together. He was also a professor who taught at the University of Wisconsin. Leopold became very famous for the work he did to protect the natural world. He taught others how to respect and protect what we've been given.

In his book *A Sand County Almanac*, Leopold wrote about the lessons he learned when he visited his cabin, the "Shack," in Sauk County. The cabin was far from any town or city. In the book, he told the story of cutting the wood of a "good oak" after it was struck by lightning. As his saw passed through each of the tree's rings, he remembered a piece of history that he had lived through. Each ring told a story about saving trees and other natural resources. Aldo Leopold used the tree to teach people lessons about protecting nature.

Today, a sign marks the place where the Good Oak once stood.

Aldo Leopold sitting in front of the Shack.

Leopold's daughter Nina nurses a young pine.

Aldo Leopold's Pine Forest

Baraboo

Scientist Aldo Leopold lived with his family in Madison during the school year. But on weekends in the summers, they spent time at the Shack. The Shack was built near the Wisconsin River in Baraboo. Once, it had been a chicken coop. The Leopold family worked together to turn it into a wilderness cabin.

Aldo Leopold takes a close look at a red pine.

Together, the family worked to restore the land around the Shack. One summer, they planted 3000 tiny pine seedlings. Each seedling is a tree that is just starting to grow. Every member of the family took part. But that year, there was no water. It was in the middle of a terrible drought called the Dust Bowl. The drought had dried up all of the lakes and rivers, and it rained very little. Their efforts failed, and the trees did not grow.

The next year, the family tried again. This time, they planted two seedlings in each hole. The family hoped one seedling out of the two would grow into a healthy tree. Then they watered each seedling with buckets of water from the pump in front of the Shack. They used a "brigade" system, which works like a relay. One person would fill the bucket with water, and then pass it on to the next person. That person would pass it to the next, all the way to where the trees stood. They watered in this way until each tree had its share.

The pines the family planted are still alive today, and the Shack is still standing. In 2009, it became a National Historic Landmark. You can visit the Shack and its pine forest at the Aldo Leopold Legacy Center in Baraboo.

John Muir's Locust

Madison

One warm spring day in 1863, a student named John Muir learned a lesson from a tree. He was studying at the University of Wisconsin. As he walked past a black locust tree on the college campus, he noticed the tree's flowers. Even though the flowers came from a tree, they looked a lot like the flowers that came from the pea plant. "But how could this be," he wondered, "when the pea is a weak, clinging plant, and the locust is a big, thorny tree?"

Just like humans, trees and plants belong to families. John Muir was fasci-

The Muir Locust in 1955.

UNIVERSITY OF WISCONSIN-EXTENSION

nated by this idea. He wanted to know how one plant was connected to another. Who were its brothers? Its sisters? Its mother? How could a tree flower be like a pea flower? All of these questions made Muir curious. He decided to make the study of nature his life's work. To celebrate that event, every time he moved to a new house, the first tree he planted was a black locust.

Do you think the pea flower and the locust flower look the same?

The original black locust stood on a hill at the University of Wisconsin until 1956. Then it was cut down because of decay. To remember the tree, letter openers and other objects were made from its wood. The college gave them away as gifts.

Many years after he went to the university, John Muir became famous. He is known across the United States for protecting and honoring our forests and wildlife. He even started a club for people who want to take good care of nature: the Sierra Club.

John Muir

Trees can be teachers and friends. They help us to remember the past, and remind us to take care of the natural world. Wisconsin's trees have many fascinating stories to tell. Do you have a tree story of your own?

MAP OF WISCONSIN TREES

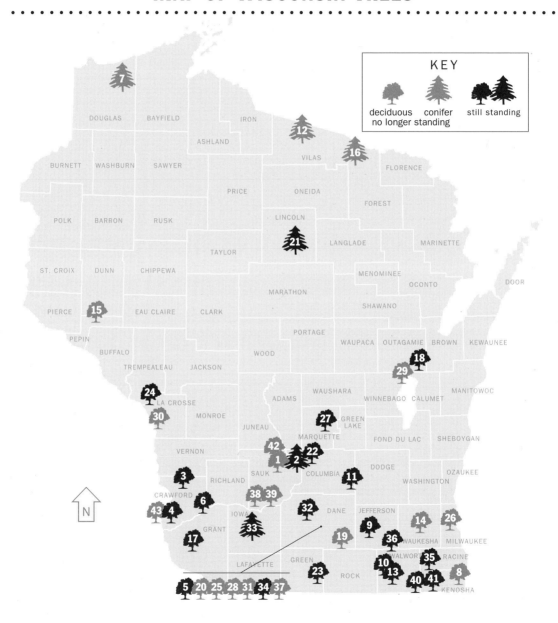

KEY

deciduous
no longer standing

conifer

still standing

DOUGLAS
BAYFIELD
IRON
ASHLAND
VILAS
FLORENCE
BURNETT WASHBURN SAWYER
PRICE
ONEIDA
FOREST
POLK BARRON RUSK
LINCOLN
LANGLADE
MARINETTE
TAYLOR
MENOMINEE
OCONTO
DOOR
ST. CROIX DUNN CHIPPEWA
MARATHON
SHAWANO
PIERCE
EAU CLAIRE CLARK
PEPIN
PORTAGE
WAUPACA OUTAGAMIE BROWN KEWAUNEE
BUFFALO
WOOD
TREMPEALEAU JACKSON
WAUSHARA
ADAMS
WINNEBAGO CALUMET MANITOWOC
LA CROSSE
MONROE
JUNEAU
GREEN LAKE
MARQUETTE
COLUMBIA
FOND DU LAC SHEBOYGAN
VERNON
SAUK
DODGE
WASHINGTON OZAUKEE
RICHLAND
CRAWFORD
IOWA
DANE
JEFFERSON
WAUKESHA MILWAUKEE
GRANT
LAFAYETTE
GREEN
ROCK
WALWORTH RACINE
KENOSHA

N

Wisconsin Trees in this Book

1. Aldo Leopold's Good Oak, *Baraboo, Sauk County*

2. Aldo Leopold's Pine Forest, *Baraboo, Sauk County*

3. Ben Logan's Big Maple, *Seneca, Crawford County*

4. Blackhawk Cottonwood, *Prairie du Chien, Crawford County*

5. Blackhawk Hickory, *Madison, Dane County*

6. Boscobel's Dean Oak, *Boscobel, Grant County*

7. Brule River White Pine, *Brule River State Forest, Douglas County*

8. The Buried Forest, *Pleasant Prairie, Kenosha County*

9. Centennial Maple, *Fort Atkinson, Jefferson County*

10. Civil War Sign-Up Tree, *Delavan, Walworth County*

11. Columbus Cottonwood, near *Columbus, Dodge County*

12. Cram/Houghton Blaze Tree, *Trout Lake, Vilas County*

13. Delavan Founder's Oak, *Delavan, Walworth County*

14. Dunbar Oak, Waukesha, *Waukesha County*

15. Durand Courthouse Hanging Tree, *Durand, Pepin County*

16. General MacArthur White Pine, *Nicolet National Forest, Forest County*

17. Grant County Sycamore, *Bloomington, Grant County*

18. Grignon Elms, *Kaukauna, Outagamie County*

19. Hanerville Oak, *Hanerville, Dane County*

20. Harvey Oak, *Madison, Dane County*

21. The Haunted Mansion and Pines, *Merrill, Lincoln County*

22. Indian Agency House and Portage Elms, *Portage, Columbia County*

23. Indian Half-Way Tree, *Brodhead, Green County*

24. Lunde Chestnut Trees, *Trempealeau, Trempealeau County*

25. Mercer's Addition Trial Marker Tree, *Madison, Dane County*

26. Milwaukee Trail Marker Tree, *Milwaukee, Milwaukee County*

27. Montello Cottonwood, *Montello, Marquette County*

28. John Muir's Locust, *Madison, Dane County*

29. Neenah Treaty Elm, *Neenah, Winnebago County*

30. Parade Day Hanging Tree, *La Crosse, La Crosse County*

31. Peck Bur Oak, *Madison, Dane County*

32. Pleasant Company Oak, *Middleton, Dane County*

33. The Poet's Larch, *Dodgeville, Iowa County*

34. President's Oak, *Madison, Dane County*

35. Rhodes Bald Cypress, *Richard Bong State Recreational Area, Racine County*

36. The Scary Oak, *Kettle Moraine State Forest, Walworth County*

37. State Street Elms, *Madison, Dane County*

38. Taliesin Elm, *Spring Green, Sauk County*

39. Tea Circle Oaks, *Spring Green, Sauk County*

40. Twin Lakes Trail Marker Tree, *Twin Lakes, Kenosha County*

41. Upside-Down Trees, *Wilmot, Kenosha County*

42. Walking Staff Tree, *Lake Delton, Sauk County*

43. Wyalusing Maple, *Wyalusing State Park, Grant County*

IDENTIFYING TREES CHART

Use this chart to find out which Wisconsin trees are in your area.

	Tree Shape	Leaf Shape	Height	Used For
American Elm	wide with spreading branches	oval, with toothy edges	11 stories	shade, borders
Bur Oak	wide with spreading branches	top is wider than bottom, with uneven lobes and smooth edges	10 stories	firewood, furniture
Common Oak	wide with spreading branches	uneven lobes and smooth edges	12 stories	furniture
Sugar Maple	oval with spreading branches	with 5 points, like your hand, and smaller points in between	10 stories	maple syrup
White Pine	tall and pointed	needles in bunches of 5	12 stories	timber

TREE TERMS

· ·

acorn: the seed of an oak tree

bark: the hard covering on the outside of a tree

burls: large knots of wood that grow on a tree when fungus gets under the bark

centennial: a 100-year-old birthday

champion tree: a tree that has the record for being the tallest or largest

chestnut blight: the disease that killed the chestnut trees

cones: the hard, woody fruit of a pine tree

conifer: a tree that has needles and cones

decay: when a tree rots or breaks down because of age or disease

deciduous tree: a tree whose leaves fall each year

drought: a long spell of very dry weather

dune: a huge hill made of sand

Dutch elm disease: the disease that killed the elm trees

elm bark beetle: the insect that carries Dutch elm disease

environment: the natural world of the land, sea, and air

forest ranger: a person who manages and protects the land in a forest

fungus: a living thing that is like a plant put has no leaves, flower, or roots

grove: a group of trees planted or growing near one another

historic site: a place you can visit where an important event took place in the past or where a famous person once lived

identification: telling one tree apart from another by its shape, leaves, and fruit

Indian agent: a person who worked for the United States government in the 1800s to help Indians and non-Indians get along

knees: woody knobs that grow up from the roots of a bald cypress tree

lumberjack: a person whose job it is to cut down trees and get them to the sawmill

monument: a statue, building, or plaque that is put up to remind people of a historic event or person

natural resource: a material found in nature that helps people live, like forests, water, or minerals

needle: a very thin, pointed leaf on a pine tree

plaque: a metal sign with words written on it, usually placed on a wall in a public place

preserve: to protect something so that it stays in its natural state

ring: the growth of a tree each year, which grows in rings from the middle of the trunk outward

root: the part of a tree or plant that grows under the ground

sapling: a young tree

scar: a wound in the bark of tree that stays with it as it grows

seedling: a tree that is just starting to grow

spring: a place where water rises up from the ground and becomes a stream

state park: a piece of land set apart by the state for everyone to use and preserve

surveyor: in the 1800s, a person who measured the size and shape land very carefully to draw maps of large areas

teeth: notches on the edge of a leaf

timber: trees that are cut down to be used for building

treaty: an agreement between two groups of people

tree doctor: a person who heals and takes care of trees for a living

trunk: the main stem of a tree

FACTS ABOUT WISCONSIN TREES

∞ Wisconsin has an amazing 2.4 billion trees.

∞ Trees cover 16 million acres of Wisconsin—nearly half of our state!

∞ Most of Wisconsin's forests are in the northern part of the state.

∞ Most of the trees you see today are less than 125 years old.

∞ Healthy trees have as many as 200,000 leaves. That's twice as many hairs as you have on your head!

∞ Trees don't just make paper and houses. Products from trees go into toothpaste, football helmets, and even milk shakes!

∞ Most trees live for about 60 years, but some can live for as long as 400.

∞ Tree roots don't grow straight down. Most grow in the top 12 inches of soil with the roots spreading out.

∞ Leaves change color in the fall because there is less daylight and because the air is colder.

∞ The most common tree in Wisconsin is the sugar maple, followed by the red pine.

Source: *Wisconsin's Forests: 2004*, Resource Bulletin NRS-23 (Newton Square, PA: United States Forest Service, 2004).

To Learn More About Wisconsin Trees

Burns, Diane. *Trees, Leaves, and Bark.* NorthWood Press, 1995.

Dorros, Arthur. *A Tree is Growing.* New York: Scholastic Press, 1997.

Florian, Douglas. *Discovering Trees.* New York: Aladdin Books, 1990.

Morrison, Gordon. *Oak Tree.* Boston: Houghton Mifflin Co., 2000.

Leopold, Aldo. *A Sand County Almanac.* 1949. New York: Oxford University Press, 2001.

Logan, Ben. *The Land Remembers.* 1975. Blue Mounds, WI: Itchy Cat Press, 2006.

Oppenheim, Joanne. *Have You Seen Trees?* New York: Scholastic, 1995.

ACKNOWLEDGMENTS

Turning the dream of this book into reality was made possible by the talented staff of the Wisconsin Historical Society Press. I gratefully acknowledge Kathy Borkowski, Director; Kate Thompson, Acquisitions Editor; Bobbie Malone, Director of School Services; Diane Drexler, Managing Editor; Sam Finesurrey, Production Assistant; and especially Sara Phillips, Developmental Editor, who expertly guided the project from manuscript to printed book. Thank you also to those outside of the Press who reviewed the manuscript and provided helpful consultation: Kathe Conn, Director of the Aldo Leopold Nature Center; Genny Fannucchi, Forest Resource Education and Awareness Specialist at the Wisconsin Department of Natural Resources; and Tessa Jilot, Outreach Specialist and Forestry Educator at the Wisconsin Department of Natural Resources. Also thanks to the children who helped choose the tree stories for this book from *Every Root an Anchor*: Stephanie Strandlie, Sydney Johnson, Molly Dougherty, Emma Davis, Ariane Poisson, Willy Bernstein, Abram Krause, and Sara Maly.

INDEX

This index points to the pages where you can read about things, persons, places, and ideas. If you do not find the word you are looking for, try to think of another word that means about the same thing.

Sometimes when you look up a word, the index will point to another word, like this: White pines. *See* Pines.

When you see a **boldface** page number, it means there is a picture or map on the page.

ABOUT THE AUTHOR

R. Bruce Allison is an arborist (tree doctor) from Madison, Wisconsin. He holds a Masters of Science in Forestry and a Doctorate in Land Resources from the University of Wisconsin–Madison. He has served as the president of the Wisconsin Arborist Association and as chairman of the Dane County Tree Board and Wisconsin Urban Forestry Council. Allison is the author of several books and articles about trees, most recently *Wisconsin's Champion Trees: A Tree Hunter's Guide* (1980; 2005) and *Every Root an Anchor: Wisconsin's Famous and Historic Trees* (Wisconsin Historical Society Press, 2005). This is his first book for children.